Reward Learning with Badges

Spark Student Achievement

Brad Flickinger

International Society for Technology in Education
EUGENE, OREGON • ARLINGTON, VIRGINIA

Reward Learning with Badges
Spark Student Achievement
Brad Flickinger

Editor: *Emily Reed*
Production Manager: *Christine Longmuir*
Copy Editor: *Kristin Landon*
Editorial Assistant: *Corinne Gould*
Book Design and Production: *Kim McGovern*

Library of Congress Cataloging-in-Publication Data available.

First Edition
ISBN: 978-1-56484-382-1
Ebook version available.

Printed in the United States of America

ISTE® is a registered trademark of the International Society for
Technology in Education.

About ISTE

The International Society for Technology in Education (ISTE) is the premier nonprofit organization serving educators and education leaders committed to empowering connected learners in a connected world. ISTE serves more than 100,000 education stakeholders throughout the world.

ISTE's innovative offerings include the ISTE Conference & Expo, one of the biggest, most comprehensive ed tech events in the world—as well as the widely adopted ISTE Standards for learning, teaching and leading in the digital age and a robust suite of professional learning resources, including webinars, online courses, consulting services for schools and districts, books, and peer-reviewed journals and publications. Visit iste.org to learn more.

Related ISTE Titles

Flip Your Classroom: Reach Every Student in Every Class Every Day, by Jonathan Bergmann & Aaron Sams

Let's Get Social: The Educator's Guide to Edmodo, by Ginger Carlson & Raphael Raphael

To see all books available from ISTE, please visit iste.org/resources

About the Author

 **Brad Flickinger** has always been a geek and a maker. His fondest childhood memories are of taking things apart and programming computers. In high school, he worked at his favorite hangout—Radio Shack, where he helped people with problems they had with electronics and early computers.

Brad began his career in the newspaper industry but when he saw the "writing on the wall" about the future of newspapers and the internet he left to pursue jobs in education and technology. Ultimately he fell in love with teaching, which he still calls his "dream job." Brad taught technology at Bethke Elementary in northern Colorado. His students produced the longest running and most popular student podcast on iTunes. His student-made movies have had over 230,000 online views, and in 2012, he received the Leadership Award from Edtech Digest for his blog SchoolTechnology.org that gets over 70,000 visitors a month.

Brad currently lives in Panama City, Panama with his wife and continues to spend his summers traveling the world as an ed tech speaker at conferences, attending district meetings, and consulting to help schools and districts do what he does so well.

Contents

Introduction

TALK TO ALMOST ANY teacher about problems in education, and you will hear some of the same issues mentioned again and again:

- The students aren't motivated. They just don't care about learning.

- They're all over the place! Some are painfully behind while others are bored.

- If only I could just work with each one individually— they just have such different needs!

- They don't see the importance of what they are learning. How can I show them the relevance?

- I just can't compete with smartphones and tablets for the students' attention. They want everything to be entertaining! They'd rather be playing a game on their phones than listening to me.

Students don't see the point in learning facts and information when they have all the information in the world at their fingertips. Why would they want to study for a quiz when they know they can just ask Siri?

I can certainly relate to most of these issues. Seven years ago, I was in what should have been my dream job as an elementary school technology teacher, but I was on the verge of quitting. I was frustrated, the students were bored, and I was turning into another cynical teacher—one who realizes that perhaps the mountain to education reform was just too big and too steep to conquer.

The Need for Change

If we do an honest evaluation of education, each dissatisfied party has a point—the frustrated teacher and the apathetic student. Education does need a change. Students *are* individuals who learn in different ways and at different paces. Technology *has* changed the expectations and skills that students bring into classrooms. Information is readily available like never before. And, for these and other reasons, many students *are* bored and unmotivated.

Many schools and districts are looking to technology as the answer, with 1:1 programs popping up across the globe, and billions of dollars being invested into technology initiatives. But, as many teachers have experienced firsthand, simply adding the technology isn't doing the trick. After the excitement of a new batch of iPads or laptops wears off, the same old problems often arise. This may be at least partly because too many schools and teachers keep on teaching just the same way as they always have. Worksheets and quizzes are reformatted into electronic versions, PowerPoint presentations replace posterboards, and research for "the big paper" happens online instead of in books.

Technology no doubt makes many of these tasks easier, and may make them somewhat more engaging for digital age students. However, the technological revolution in education that has transpired over the last 12 years should do more than change the way students take quizzes and present the facts they learn—it should be changing *what* they learn, *how* they learn, and the way learning is demonstrated and evaluated. Unfortunately, we have students who think that technology is only for entertainment and teachers who think technology is only good for looking up facts.

I have seen students in a "high-tech" middle school filling out an online quiz about the rivers of South America from memory. The very devices they were using to take these quizzes could have instantly provided not only the name of the river they were now trying to recall and regurgitate, but also countless statistics about the river, information about the country and continent in which the river exists, images and video of the river, and even connection with people who live or work near the river.

In short, facts are free and easy to get. Education no longer needs to serve the function of transferring factual information into students' minds. This doesn't mean teachers and education are no longer necessary. In fact, I would argue it has become a lot more important—and a lot more fun. We now have the task of guiding students through the renaissance of learning.

So, as it turned out, I realized I didn't need to quit teaching—I just needed to quit teaching the way I had always done it. I needed to rethink everything. And when I did, my badge system was born.

The Vision

I started by reimagining what type of students I wanted to see emerging from my classroom. Of course, there is not one singular purpose to education, but what I landed on was this: I wanted to give students opportunities to find their passions in order to become productive members of society.

In order to prepare them to contribute to society, they needed to have the type of thinking skills that allow students to thrive in their educational future and beyond. Just as basic, factual knowledge is no longer the sole trait that distinguishes teachers from students, factual knowledge is also no longer enough to set apart an educated individual in the work force. Students needed to be able to think creatively, and they needed specific, demonstrable digital age skills. They needed to excel at the higher end of Bloom's taxonomy, which I know is not a new idea. But now more than ever, independent and creative thinking may be among the highest currencies a student, or a potential employee, could possess.

I also wanted my students to be able to point to concrete skills that they had proven. Being able to show an employer a straight-A report card is certainly nice, but this doesn't attest to exactly what students can do. In some cases, all it suggests is a certain amount of seat time, a strong memory, and a knack for following directions. I wanted my students to walk out of my classroom with an arsenal of technology skills that were applicable in the real world.

Finally, I also wanted my students to be passionate about learning itself, and about whatever they discovered their own niche to be. As discussed at the beginning of this chapter, though, "passionate" might be the last word that teachers would use to describe their students. So what do modern students need to discover a passion in school? Research shows that this new crop of students is mainly motivated by three things: choice, effort and persistence (Bhoje, 2015).

So, I designed a system that gave students a great deal of choice within a clear framework. It put the student in the driver's seat in many areas of their education, including how they would spend their class time, which skills they would learn when, and how they would demonstrate what they learned. As Lee Crockett wrote in *Literacy Is Not Enough,* "To help our students make a successful transition from school to life, we must shift the responsibility of learning from the teacher, where it has traditionally been, to the learners, where it belongs" (Crockett, Jukes, & Churches, 2011).

I also designed my system with high standards that required and recognized real effort and persistence. This might seem counterintuitive, when we see so many students struggling with their current educational expectations, but the key to engaging students might actually be to make the material *more* challenging. Students truly, deep down inside of themselves, do not want success in school to be easy to earn. They want it to require some persistence—this is what gets the respect of their peers.

Even with choice and challenge, students also need to see the meaning and value in what they are learning. I wanted my students to see how they could use the skills from my class to make a difference in the world. This did sound a bit idealistic at first, but I found a way to incorporate it into my badge system, and it has engaged students like nothing else. When students immediately saw how they could apply the skills they were learning to change the world, they became the passionate learners I had dreamed of. In fact, they became so engaged that they were doing a majority of the work for my class on their own time, outside of class, of their own volition. And, in addition to this overall spike in motivation, I also did had several students discover a passion that they never would have outside of this system. I'll share a few of the success stories later. First, though, I want to introduce some of the educational philosophies and movements that helped to inspire and inform my badge system.

CHAPTER ONE

Inspiration for the Badge System

OF COURSE, I AM well aware that I am not the first educator to have the epiphany that things need to change. Educators are innovators, and the past decade has seen many promising ideas for rethinking education. My system stands on the shoulders of several different theories, methods, and movements, and as you read about my badge system, you may recognize some elements and practices. Just in case you aren't familiar with any of these terms (and also so you know that I didn't just pull my crazy ideas out of thin air), I'll give a very brief summary of some of my sources of inspiration. My badge system arose amidst this "perfect storm" of ideas.

Influential Books

Literacy Is Not Enough:
21st Century Fluencies for the Digital Age

When Lee Crockett, Ian Jukes, and Andrew Churches published this book in 2011, I had already embarked on the creation of my badge program. Nonetheless, their work had a major impact on my teaching. First, we seemed to be on the same page about the way education needed to go. Second, they did an excellent job of articulating the exact ways and reasons that education needs to change. While technology is mentioned often, the authors focus heavily on the ways students need to think to be successful in the digital age. The ideas of flexibility, creativity, problem solving, and collaboration are touched on repeatedly, which gave me encouragement that I was on the right track. It also frequently put into words frustrations and the goals that I was grappling with that were sometimes difficult to articulate.

Flip Your Classroom:
Reach Every Student in Every Class Every Day

Jonathan Bergmann and Aaron Sams certainly appealed to teachers with the promising subtitle to their 2012 book. What teacher doesn't wish to reach every student in every class every day? With the recognition that information is easily accessible outside of the classroom, they proposed that the classroom should no longer be the place where knowledge is acquired. Instead, students could be introduced to concepts, lessons, and facts on their own, through video tutorials. Students could watch the videos at home—as quickly or slowly as they wanted, with as many pauses and replays as necessary. They realized that the part of the learning process that the teacher was most needed for was when students began trying to use the knowledge in practice problems or experiments.

The classroom, then, could become the place where students analyzed, used, tested, played with, and reacted to the information they had learned. Instead of giving information in the classroom and asking students to practice it outside of class, students could come to class with the basic facts in place and delve into higher-order thinking and processing with their teachers and peers. So, instead of functioning as fact dispensers, teachers and students get to share in the more dynamic aspects of learning, which is a win on both of their parts. Practitioners of this system report enjoying far more interaction with their students, fewer classroom management issues, more engaged students, and more success in individualizing education. The original authors later implemented a mastery approach to their flipped classroom model, in which students can navigate the flipped classroom model at their own pace. With the flipped model of instruction being so very untraditional, it is sometimes hard to then try and assign traditional letter grades to the learning that is occurring, which is why some have called my badges the perfect assessment tool for the flipped classroom model.

Learning Models and Approaches

What if, instead of working toward a test or a report, students were working on something authentic and meaningful? In project-based learning, students are challenged to solve real-world problems with projects that have authentic audiences. This type of learning, when well executed, helps students see the relevance of their studies and connects them to their communities and worlds. No longer is education a result of secretive transactions of manufactured assignments between teachers and students. Instead, students are challenged to gain knowledge for the purpose of solving a meaningful problem. In addition, instead of passively responding to the questions that a teacher poses, students in project-based learning are helping to formulate the questions. I love the independence, meaning, and authenticity of the project-based approach, and I strove to incorporate all of these elements into my badge system.

Challenge-Based Learning

Even the tech company Apple has weighed in with a fresh approach to education with a strategy called Challenge-Based Learning. This approach shares a great deal with the general concept of problem-based learning, but, unsurprisingly, it is much more tied to technology. In their classroom guide to Challenge-Based Learning, they reiterate the problem at hand like this: "Today's students are presented with content-centric assignments that meet standards but lack a real-world context and opportunities for education" (Apple Inc., 2010). In response, they propose that students' learning mirror the modern workplace, as they work collaboratively to address real-world problems using technology. After being exposed to a real and current issue facing their community, such as an environmental threat or a social problem, students are challenged to formulate a meaningful response with guidance from their teacher. It was important when designing my badges system that I include a challenge for each badge, something that the students will find interesting enough for them to be motivated to pursue.

Gamification

If you've ever watched the focus and dedication of a young person playing a video game that they are invested in, you've probably wished you could capture just a fraction of that focus and attention. As the Education Lab at MIT observed, "Game players regularly exhibit persistence, risk taking, attention to detail, and problem solving, all behaviors that would ideally be regularly demonstrated in school" (Klopfer, Osterweil, & Salen, 2009). Out of desire to connect these traits to education, it has been proposed that education itself be "gamified." Gamification has been around as a concept for a long time, but the word was not largely used until in 2002, when Nick Pelling, a computer game developer, started giving it some traction.

When I first heard this term, I panicked, thinking that people wanted to turn my classroom into a video game, but I soon found out that this was not the case. Gamification, as applied to education, applies video-game design concepts to educational concepts. Some of the most commonly applied concepts include the idea of charting progress via levels, points, and achievements, as video games commonly do. Instead of completing a unit, students can "level up" and unlock new achievements. A course takes on the feeling of a unified quest, and each new skill they learn is both earning them points and moving them toward completion of their larger mission.

It is important to note that in my system the badge should only be part of the motivation. As in game play, a badge is just a marker—a way to keep track of where you've been and to show others your skill level. You don't play a video game just to get a badge—you play because you enjoy the game, and the badges and points are rewards along a journey. With each badge earned, your body gets a shot of dopamine (the reward hormone), which keeps you coming back for more. Badges are a way to literally keep score. For a badge to have true value, it needs to be hard to earn. There is a fine balance between not hard enough and too hard, something that took a little testing with my students. While it is true that my level 1 badges are relatively easy—students get a taste of early success—the higher-level badges get harder as they progress. This gives my badges "street-cred" among students. When my students see that a peer has the filmmaking badge (level 4), they know how hard that badge is to get, so there is some respect given to the badge earner.

Figure 1.1 Students display badges they have earned on their backpacks

The Hacker Mindset

While not its own educational philosophy, the "hacker mindset" is important for teachers to understand, and it too has its origins in video games. Students who think like a hacker are the ones who look for shortcuts, ways to improve, and solutions that no one has tried before. Hackers also give back—they love to share and teach what they've just learned to other in their community, which is why videos that show game-hacks are so popular. As a technology teacher I love it when my students figure out a better way and then teach me, because when the student becomes the teacher, you know that deeper learning has just occurred.

As part of my research into gamification, I started to play a few video games, and the first one I tried was called Cut the Rope. I was impressed with how the game taught me as I progressed through the levels—what is referred to as "just in time" learning. The game taught me only what I needed to know for the next task I was to accomplish, and over time my skills built one on another until I became quite good at the game. I was in a cycle of learning and immediately using skills, and I was becoming a Cut the Rope champ. The game wouldn't have been much fun if I had been forced to sit around and learn all of the skills and theory before I could start on the game's objective, and the game creators recognized this. Instead, they spread the skill lessons throughout the quest, strategically placed ahead of the challenges that required them.

This is the approach that many of our students bring (or would like to bring) to learning. This means that if I tell a kid to play a song on the guitar, they go online and looks up which chords are used for that song. Then, they will go to YouTube and search "How to play a C-chord on a guitar," watch a 3-minute video, and within minutes, they are playing a C-chord. Soon, they're playing the song. They don't want to sit down and learn every chord and note before they play their first song—they want to gain the knowledge as they need it. Furthermore, students with this mindset may be loath to learn skills in isolation without an immediate application.

Some have even adopted the term "hackschooling" to describe an alternative approach to education outside of the classroom. In his TEDx Talk, "Hackschooling Makes Me Happy," (youtube.com/watch?v=h11u3vtcpaY), 13-year-old Logan LaPlante describes the hacker mindset in education as "opportunistic." It doesn't commit to a single curriculum, but instead remains flexible enough to take advantage of any learning opportunities or questions that arise. Using the metaphor of a snow-covered mountain, he explains, "If everyone skied this mountain like most people think of education, everyone would be skiing the same line—probably the safest—and the rest of the powder would go untouched. I look at this and see a thousand possibilities ... skiing, to me, is freedom, and so is my education (TEDx, 2013)." As a teacher, I don't necessarily advocate ditching the school system, but I do believe that the elements of the hacking mindset, such as choice, flexibility, and "just in time" learning, can be applied in the traditional classroom.

The Growth Mindset

Stanford researcher Carol Dweck spent years exploring what makes people successful, and her findings have significant implications for education. She explains that most people's mindsets about success fall into one of two categories: fixed mindset or growth mindset.

Those who have a fixed mindset assume that each individual possesses a certain fixed degree of intelligence and ability. In the same way that some people are tall and some are short, one's intelligence is a set quantity that won't really change throughout life. Education, then, is simply the process of documenting or demonstrating how much intelligence and talent one has. Few people might immediately admit to this mindset, but we hear it often in education. Parents may say their child just "isn't a reader," as if the skill is a have or have-not proposition. Students often decide they are bad at certain subjects and lose motivation to try because they feel they've gotten to the end of their fixed ability and can go no further. Grading is often a one-shot transaction, where a student makes an attempt, a teacher assigns a grade, and that's the end of it.

A growth mindset, on the other hand, sees intelligence and ability as dynamic traits that can be developed through education and experience. Natural gifts or talents are only the starting point from which an individual begins the journey of growth and learning. Education, then, is a series of opportunities to stretch and strengthen one's intelligence and skills. Not surprisingly, this mindset is far more likely to lead to success in education and in life. In fact, Dweck identified the difference in mindset as one of the key predictors of success.

Why does the mindset make such a difference? Think about how each mindset would lead a student to view challenges and obstacles. Someone with a growth mindset would see them as opportunities to learn something new as they face new circumstances and experiment with different solutions. Sure, they might not figure it out right away, and they may experience some frustration, but ultimately, they believe success is attainable by embracing challenges. Those with a fixed mindset, in comparison will avoid challenges and give up quickly. Each challenge threatens to expose their shortcomings, and an unsuccessful first attempt is interpreted as failure.

Similarly, effort is always worthwhile for those who believe they have the potential to grow, but seems pointless for those who feel that that each task only tests their innate ability. If a teacher corrects or criticizes a student with a growth mindset, it can be interpreted as a contribution to their constant growing process. To a student with a fixed mindset, though, criticism tells them their fixed ability isn't good enough. To a student with a growth mindset, another student's success can demonstrate what is possible. In a fixed mindset, though, the success of others is a threat. If someone else is succeeding, they are demonstrating their superior fixed abilities, which can only serve to make others look and feel worse by comparison.

As you might have guessed, the badge program promotes the growth mindset. It recognizes that learning is a process, and while each student will explore at a different pace, learning is attainable for everyone. It emphasizes skills that can be developed through practice, trial and error. If a student doesn't create a successful animation the first time they try, it doesn't mean they're incapable of doing it—it means that they will have to use resources, confer with others, and work hard until they succeed. The feedback cycle, as you will see, allows for continued revision and improvement until a skill is mastered, perpetuating the idea that assessment is meant to develop—not measure—students' abilities.

Design Thinking

Design thinking has its origins outside of the realm of education, but its potential as an educational framework has recently been explored in the classroom with promising potential. This term originated as a name for the type of problem-solving skills used in fields such as engineering, architecture, and urban planning. It emphasizes outside-of-the-box thinking and creativity in response to open-ended or even undefined problems. Instead of following a set, analytical process, it relies on a much more creative and open thinking model. Though the concept can be a bit amorphous, it is often broken down into several stages. Though these are sometimes phrased differently, or broken into more parts, I like the division into five stages: empathize, define, ideate, prototype, and test.

Instead of presenting students with a neat, concrete question, design thinking would have students start by coming to understand, or empathize with, a certain challenging situation. Then, it is the students' jobs to clearly define the specific problem, or problems, that need to be addressed. These are steps that teachers often do for the students as they create assignments, but it is a valuable and realistic part of many real-world problem-solving situations that students need to experience. Once the task at hand has been established, it's time to ideate. This step involves creative brainstorming and isn't limited to a single subject area—it should be interdisciplinary and draw on the background knowledge of many different individuals. Once there are a wealth of options to discuss and work with, students can select one or more potential solutions to move into the prototype phase. Once the prototype is developed, it can be tested and refined as much as needed, and possibly even discarded and restarted.

Though the badge program doesn't necessarily walk students through this process step by step, its ideals of creative thinking, brainstorming, and continually reworking and trying new solutions do resonate with the tenets of design thinking.

Badges

My research into gamification took me in many different directions, but what really intrigued me was the use of badges to show students' competencies. Badges are the reward system used by many video games to show the players' progression toward completing certain tasks. They are specific to the skills attained, and often visually symbolic of the accomplishment. A player can amass these badges as they move throughout game play.

Badges, obviously, are not exclusive to video games. Perhaps one of the most well-known users of badges are the Boy and Girl Scouts of America. They currently offer more than 100 beautifully designed badges that represent practical, proven skills. Anyone can see at a glance that a scout has mastered canoeing, painting, or safety. Scouts have some degree of choice in the badges they choose to pursue, and through the program, they gain exposure and competency in a wide variety of skills. The visibility, symbolism, design, and structure of the Scouting program all helped to inspire my program.

More recently, digital badge programs have grown in popularity. Mozilla's Open Badges program is probably among the most well-known hubs for digital badge transactions and display. They facilitate the display of digital badges that represent all of an individual's proven skills—whether they were acquired inside or outside of a classroom (their work has mostly been with colleges and universities). Open Badges allows a variety of institutions, including the Open Badges site itself, to award badges which can then be displayed by the students and professionals on the site. Each badge is meaningful and credible because it carries with it the data of where and when it was earned and what criteria were required to earn it. It can also be linked to evidence of the skill itself, such as a website the user designed or a video they created. Their design is meant to acknowledge the fact that learning occurs beyond the classroom, and that many of the valued skills today might not appear on a typical transcript.

Figure 1.2 Merit badges are used to represent achievement among Boy Scouts and Girl Scouts.

Badges are the hallmark of a larger trend that employers are starting to demand and now universities are scrambling to deliver. I noticed a hint of this trend a few years ago when I sat in on the interviews for new teachers at our elementary school. I noticed that most of the résumés of the candidates that we were being interviewed were "skills-based" rather than traditional. Résumés that focused on skills over experience and education. More and more employers are wanting to know what skills you can bring to the job rather than what diplomas and awards you can hang on the wall. To fill this demand, universities like Carnegie Mellon have started to offer micro-credentials to their students (Digital Promise, 2015). Micro-credentials are bite-sized projects that are competency based, which allow students to gain a broad range of skills to go with their traditional degrees. These micro-credential programs are tracked by, you guessed it, badges.

 TOOLS: Resources for Creating Badges

- 1" buttons can be made easily and inexpensively using a button maker, found at craft stores or online (americanbuttonmachines.com).

- Free clipart wesbites such as classroomclipart.com or the free clipart index from Discovery Education (discoveryeducation.com) can provide designs and inspiration for badge artwork.

- For something more professional, try your local print shop or an online designer such as those found on Etsy or fiverr.com.

For the younger students that I teach, physical badges work great. They are tangible and immediate, not to mention inexpensive and easy to make. However, digital badges have a lot to offer as well, and depending on your students and school, they may be the answer for you. It certainly makes sense to promote technology skills through a digital badge system. And, depending on how you design your platform, your students' badges could be visible and useful beyond the classroom.

First, you need a platform for all of your badge-distribution needs—a place to design digital badges, describe the criteria for earning them, and, best of all, award the badges to students and see students' badges displayed.

Credly, Badge List, ClassBadges, and Mozilla Open Badges are four of the websites that are worth exploring. All of them allow you to create an account and begin designing digital badges. There is still a visual element to these badges, as each one requires an image or symbol. Some sites offer an array of images and also allow you to upload your own. One thing that really sets digital badges apart from physical badges, though, is the fact that they can carry significant information. When you design a badge, you can name it and input a description of the skills or accomplishments that the badge represents, who awarded the badge, and when the badge was awarded. So, in a digital badge system, someone looking at the animation badge would not just see a circle with a picture of a paintbrush on it. They would also see that the badge was for Animation 1, that it was awarded by Mr. Flickinger, Technology Manager at The Metropolitan School in Panama, that it was awarded on March 16, 2016, and that to earn it, the student had to demonstrate the ability to animate fluid motion and create a 30-second original animation. Impressive, right? This allows students looking back at their badges to recall their accomplishment, helps other educators to better grasp what students have done, and also lets students share their badges with the world, if desired.

Some learning management systems like Edmodo and Schoology now have badges within their ecosystem, which allows teachers to design and assign badges to projects.

All badge platforms allow badge earners to display their badges on the site itself, and the level of privacy can be determined by the instructor. Students are also able to share badges on a variety of social media and networking sites if they choose to do so. This means that students can display their skills to be seen by a wider audience, including prospective colleges or employers.

Schools aren't the only ones interested in badges, either. These sites are meant to "knit your skills together," as the Open Badges home page describes it. Credly lists a wide variety of institutions that use their digital credentials to verify achievements, including Yale, the YMCA, the National Park Service, museums, professional training organizations, and employers. Your classroom could be just the beginning of a digital badge collection that evidences a lifetime of learning.

Regardless of how your students will display their badges, physically or digitally, my system remains the same. You just need to find the type of badge display that works for you and your students. In some cases, that might mean a little of both. Some teachers have opted to use a badge management system like Badge List to track all the badges and physical badges for the students to show off their accomplishments "offline," as it were.

Technology Standards

In addition to the badges themselves, my badge system also involves a new framework for planning a unit or a course. If we simply swap badges for grades, we are not providing the paradigm shift that digital-age students need. The goals of my badge program and the reasoning behind them dovetail with the International Society for Technology in Education (ISTE) Standards for Students (formerly the NETS).

One of the main goals of my badge program is to create empowered learners. I want to see students in the driver's seat of their education, making choices and taking ownership of what they learn. But this empowerment shouldn't stop at the classroom door. Students' education should empower them to make changes in the real world. As I designed my badge program, I intentionally built in opportunities for students to use technology as a tool to change the world. The artifacts and culminating projects can—and I would argue, should—be designed to make a real impact on a local or global level. Some examples might include fundraising, raising awareness for a cause, event planning, or other charitable activities. This empowerment can be life-changing for students, both as learners and as citizens of the world.

In order to have this world-changing impact, students also need to be creators and communicators. In a world where people feel a sense of accomplishment from "liking" or retweeting a positive message, we need young people who will take innovative action to create their own powerful messages. Instead of simply being consumers and receivers of the messages, videos, and stories that already exist, students should have the ability to bring their own meaningful ideas to life. To make sure their voices are heard, they need to learn how to speak so the world will listen. This means creating high-quality technology products with substantial messages. It means researching, performing, editing, illustrating, speaking, and designing based on sound principles, but with the doors of creativity wide open. It also means completing work that will be heard and seen by real audiences, from their classmates and school to wider online audiences.

With the ability to connect to worldwide audiences, global collaboration is another essential skill that digital-age students should be introduced to. As students are encouraged to become communicators, they will see that their messages can transcend national borders. Activities such as blogging, Skyping, and working with e-pals easily connect students with a diverse range of people. When students are required to share their work with the world, the world just might respond. This isn't a possibility when technology assignments are a narrow transaction between student and teacher. The badge program is meant to open up the lines of communication between students and their world. This happens both through the sharing of work with a real-world audience and by requiring research and interaction on an international scale.

On the slightly less idealistic and more foundational level, we also need to help students become safe, savvy, and responsible users of technology. Before they begin sharing their inspired creations with the world, they need to have a sound grasp of technology best practices. Today's students are all digital students, and we have the task of guiding them as they navigate all of the opportunities and pitfalls that technology offers. From the basics of internet safety to the gray areas of copyright laws to the management of one's online reputation, there are so many important topics that often get overlooked in schools. A badge program can easily, and should, incorporate all of these skills. And, as students become creators and communicators, they also gain empathy and identification with other creators of online material. This naturally leads them to develop respect for other people's creations and opinions. As they become empowered students, they realize the great potential for good that technology has, helping them rise above the level of mindless, or even negative, uses of technology.

Still in the practical realm, the badge program also aims to help students manage, manipulate, and interpret the vast amount of information at their fingertips. As discussed earlier, the challenge facing today's students isn't accessing information. Instead, it is learning to find, select, store, use, break down, and share information in meaningful ways. Students need the tools to conduct effective online research and to catalog their resources in an organized way, both for themselves and others. They also need the means to work with data to record and present it in a way that makes sense. The badge program equips students to make information and technology work for their purposes.

CHAPTER TWO

Overview of the Badge System

NOW THAT YOU HAVE an understanding of where the inspiration for my badge system came from, you are probably wondering what the badge system is. This chapter gives an overview of the system, how it works, what it does and doesn't do.

Who Is the Badge System For?

I originally developed this system for my elementary-level technology classes, but with thoughtful adaptation, I believe it can be used for almost any subject at any grade level. It could be implemented by an entire school, by a department, or by a lone renegade teacher who wants to try something new. It is a system that can, and probably should, be eased into slowly, so even one unit within one class could be a good place to start.

The badge system was first conceived and implemented with technology education at its heart, and that is where I have experience using it. Tech teachers were also the first audience with whom I shared the system. However, I have more recently presented to teachers of different levels and different subjects, and these pioneers have adapted the system to reap similar benefits. The expansion beyond the tech classroom is still rather new, but the possibilities are exciting. You will notice that many examples throughout the book are technology based, but they should still provide an understanding of a framework that could be applied elsewhere. Ultimately, every teacher who implements the badge systems will be designing a unique program for their students, as you will see.

What the Badge System Isn't

My badge system is not a curriculum—I will not be telling you what to teach. Your content is still up to you and your school. In fact, part of what makes it so exciting is its adaptability to different content.

It's also not simply a replacement for letter grades. When I began this program, I did not keep the same course structure, lesson plans and assessments. As you will see, badges are only the tip of the iceberg—visual representations of a class that has been designed in a new way.

Teachers may want to explore digital badges, create videos of their badge challenges, and track goals and progress in Google Classroom, Edmodo, or another online platform. I believe that technology and badging go hand in hand, and I will use many examples involving technology to show this—first, because that is the subject that I teach, and second, because more and more teachers are being given technology tools with the expectation that they put them to use. However, vast technology resources are not required for a badge system to work.

What Is the Badge System?

The Badges

Badges themselves—whether mini-buttons that can be pinned onto students' backpacks, digital badges that can be displayed electronically, or "Tech-ttoos" (removable stickers that can be applied to their laptops and tablets)—are the basis of this program. Students are awarded badges for the demonstrated mastery of a specific set of skills. In my tech classes, for example, students can earn badges for podcasting, animation, filmmaking, and so on. Students may acquire content and demonstrate knowledge as a part of attaining the badge, but badges must be awarded for demonstration of skills.

The reason for the emphasis on skills over content is twofold. First, the badges are meant to be displayed publicly. If I were awarding badges based on knowledge as demonstrated by quizzes or other traditional measures, displaying badges would be akin to publishing my grade book. When I award badges for skills, however, I am making all badges attainable for any student who puts forth the effort to learn a skill. Having diverse skill sets is something that can be celebrated among students, rather than compared in a "have" and "have-not" fashion.

Second, skill-based badges reflect what I see as the new purpose of education, as mentioned earlier. Knowledge is free and readily attainable, so I wanted to shift the focus from what students *know* to what students can *do* with their knowledge.

I considered a few different options before settling on the mini-buttons to use with my third through fifth grade students. These 1-inch buttons ended up being the perfect choice because they are quite inexpensive and can easily be customized with symbols that represent students' classroom achievements. They are also easily displayed on students' back-packs, which they have with them every day. Students don't have to remember to bring them or wear them, but they are still in the students' possession, as opposed to on a classroom chart or display. Younger students also aren't able to create social media accounts, which reduces the appeal of electronic badges for them. If you teach older students, electronic badges may be the way to go.

Having a visible badge system is a must for this system, though, whether electronic or physical. First, the badges are a motivational tool for students. Students receive a tangible indicator that they have learned a skill. Achievements aren't secret transactions between the teacher and the student—they are physically awarded and visible to others. In my school, all students display their badges on their backpacks. As students progress through my class, they can literally watch their arsenal of skills grow as they attain badges.

Figure 2.1 A student's backpack adorned with badges they have earned

This visibility to others allows another advantage—everyone within a school can be aware of which students have achieved which skills. Furthermore, teachers can draw on these skills without having expertise in those areas themselves! This facilitates interdisciplinary communication and skill application. For example, during a science lesson, a teacher who sees that many of her students have achieved their Animation badge from tech class could now require that skill be used in an upcoming assignment. During a language arts lesson, a teacher could ask those who have achieved their Editing badge to serve as proofreaders for others. If a student who has a Leadership badge is seen excluding someone from a group, they can be held accountable by pointing out that their badge shows they should know better. Students and teachers can see each student's unique mix of skills and draw on the student for help, suggest the student draw on existing skills, and hold them accountable for what they have shown they can do.

Finally, these badges did eventually replace traditional letter grades in my class, which does a great service to both students and teachers. First, badges are awarded in an "all or nothing" fashion. A student either meets all the badge requirements, or they don't. For the student, this means that each badge represents an accomplishment to be proud of. Instead of turning in a sloppy project, earning a 70%, and feeling less-than confident in her mastery of the skill, a student using the badge system would be sent back to improve until she can demonstrate success. There is no squeaking by with a 60% under the badge system. If a student needs to spend more time mastering fewer skills, so be it. I would rather have my students feel 100% competent in a few skills than 60% competent in many. Please note that many teachers simply add the badge system to their traditional letter grades. Letter grades are given for knowledge and badges for skills. For example, an animation about the California Gold Rush might earn a fourth grade student a B+ for the knowledge presented and the Animation 2 badge for demonstrated mastery of animation skills.

As you'd imagine, using badge achievement as an assessment tool can be a huge relief for teachers, too. When you design a badge challenge, you will decide ahead of time what type of artifact would demonstrate mastery of the chosen skills and knowledge of content, and what requirements that artifact needs to meet, in checklist form. Then, when it comes time to assess whether the student has mastered the skill, there's no quibbling over whether to take off a point here or there, mark four or five on the rubric, or grade on a curve. If the student meets all expectations, you simply check all the boxes, and they have earned one skill on their way to a badge. If they don't meet the expectations, I simply give them the necessary feedback and they go back to work until they do. And, as a bonus, since students are working on different skills at different paces, you will never again face the dreaded experience of taking home a giant stack of almost identical papers over the weekend!

Theme and Culminating Event

Badges provide some motivation, but the best learning happens when students are intrinsically motivated. Two elements that have been game changers in my badge program have been the theme and the culminating event. The theme is the subject or content the badges are centered around. My badges represented technology skills and were grouped under the theme "Technology as a Tool." The culminating event is an opportunity to demonstrate skills earned to an authentic audience or use them for a specific purpose. At the culminating event for my badge challenge, the Kids Can Make a Difference Festival, students demonstrate, perform, or exhibit to our community what they have learned in the badge program. Instead of taking a test that prove they can regurgitate information, students must quite literally stand and deliver to prove that they "get it." The money we raise at this event goes to the charities that they students are working with. To me, this is a more authentic assessment of student learning.

By choosing a meaningful theme and culminating event, I provided students with an immediate, tangible purpose for every skill they learned. Even more importantly, the students were actually making a difference in the world as they learned. When they realized what they were doing, they were driven to learn like never before.

Structure

One of the most significant ways my teaching changed when I implemented the badge system was the shift away from a linear course structure that every student completes at the same pace. Instead, students have some degree of choice over which skills they will pursue first. They have a menu of badge challenges to pursue, with a list of one or more skills required to achieve each badge, and they can decide which badge to work on first, and which skill to begin with. (The badges can be arranged in levels, though, to prevent students from trying to pursue a complex, high-level badge before mastering the basics.) As you'll see in the step-by-step description, upfront work by the teacher makes it possible for students to access all learning resources independently. They don't have to wait until the teacher teaches the lesson about online research—the lesson already exists and is accessible to students when they need it.

Most of us default to the traditional method of asking all students to learn the same skills at the same time at the same pace. Some mention has already been made of the difficulties of trying to get 20 or 30 unique students to track at the same pace. In addition to pacing issues, there is also the question of resources and materials. If every student in class is supposed to be working on the same skill at once, every student will need the computer/ camera/ book/ resource at the same time. If students are working on different skills at different times, fewer resources can go a long way.

But the best part by far in this structure shift is the ownership and motivation that arises from students taking control of their own learning. Students do not have the option of acting as passive receivers of information in my classroom, because they are asked to take initiative and make choices when they walk in the door each day. I no longer hear the ubiquitous question "What are we doing today?" because students are now empowered to answer that question for themselves.

As a teacher, my day looks completely different in a badge system classroom than it did before. Students are spread throughout the room, working independently and collaboratively on their various badges. Now, instead of standing in the front and "performing," trying to get every student to pay attention to me at once, I have the privilege of moving from group to group, answering questions, providing guidance, and hearing about all of the awesome, creative projects my students are dreaming up. Even though I'm not the focus of the classroom, I have never felt like I have been more helpful or had stronger interactions with my students than I do within this system.

CHAPTER THREE

How Does the Badge System Work?

NOW THAT YOU HAVE a general idea of how my badge classroom differs from a traditional classroom, let's take a look at exactly how this system plays out, step by step, as a student would see it. The purpose of this chapter is to describe how the system functions. Advice, tips, and instructions on setting up your own badge system will follow in Chapters 5 and 6.

Big Picture Overview

At the beginning of a course, semester, or unit, I present students with the overall, driving theme. They find out what the overarching question being studied is, and they also learn about a culminating event or project that all of the smaller pieces will be building toward. In the case of my class, the overall theme is "Technology as a Tool," and the overarching question is, "How can we use technology to make our world better?" Students are then introduced to the selected charity for their grade level, and the culminating event is a fundraising event for that charity. Every skill and badge that students would work on throughout the year could somehow be contributed toward that final fundraising event that is held near the end of each school year.

A teacher could develop the theme of "Math in the Real World." The overarching question could be something like, "How can banks and credit card companies help or hurt someone financially?"

Introduction of Badges

To start, my students simply log onto their Google Classroom accounts and join a particular badge challenge using the join code that I have provided. (Chapter 5 goes into details on how each badge challenge is created.)

Then, once they are in Google Classroom class, they are presented with all of the badges that can be pursued throughout the upcoming unit or course, along with the skills that are needed to achieve each one. Earning a badge requires the mastery of one or more skills. Badges are organized into levels, and students must start at level 1. These badges will probably include the most foundational skills to success within the unit or course. For example, in my tech class, the first level 1 badge is called Tech Basics. To earn it, students must demonstrate skills in online safety, and prove that they understand the rules with regard to the technology that they get to use in the school. Other badges in my level 1 include Keyboarding, Digital Portfolio and Email. Students can decide which badge and skill they want to pursue first and spend as much or as little time as they need to demonstrate mastery of that skill. For example, one student might earn their keyboarding badge in 15 minutes because they can easily prove mastery, where another student might take four weeks or longer because they needed time to increase their keyboarding speed and accuracy.

The Badge Challenge

Once a student has selected which badge they will pursue and which skill they will attempt first, they will receive the "challenge" for that badge. Each challenge is tied to the narrative of the theme, and they need to know what skills they are pursuing, why it is important, and what artifact they will need to create to earn their badge. For my students, the challenge is usually presented in a short video in which I explain the skills and their importance and then basically dare them to do some great work. A challenge could also be delivered in writing, either electronically or on paper. However, I do like the way I can convey my enthusiasm for the challenge via video, and I recommend giving that method a try. My video for the Level 2, Audio 1 badge explains how they will learn the basics of audio production by creating a 60-second commercial not only to bring awareness to the charity but also to get people to attend the fundraising festival. After this short video, they'll know why the skill is important and what is expected of them.

Student Examples

When expectations are set at a high level, students need to know that it is not impossible to meet them. For this reason, the first thing I show the students after the badge challenge is a student example—proof that someone else, a student their age—has indeed met this challenge. Now, they have something to aspire to, or even something to top. When I first develop a badge, I will give it to a few students to try out. These are my beta-testers—they give me feedback on my tutorials and they create the first student examples for the rest to follow, such as this example of a student-created video from the Animation 2 badge (vimeo.com/158982937). Each year I update my examples for each badge with the best from that year. This process keeps raising the bar of the challenge.

Tutorials

This is the step in which the instructions and content necessary for a student to master a skill are delivered. However, since each student will be working on different skills at a different pace, this delivery will not come from the front of the classroom. This is where the flipped classroom influence really comes through. Students will independently access whatever the teacher has prepared as tutorials. These may include ready-made resources, such as a Kahn Academy or YouTube video or a podcast. It could also include an article or set of instructions they need to read. Or, once again, a self-made video, screencast, presentation, or podcast might serve this function. I often use a simply over-the-shoulder shot of myself walking through a skill step by step and narrating as I go. As you will see with this tutorial I created for the Animation 2 badge, I just shoot it with a camera over my shoulder (vimeo.com/158984029). Multiple tutorial resources can be provided for a single skill, which I often do.

The students can access these tutorials whenever they need to, and rewatch, reread, or listen to them as often as needed. For example, in my bouncing ball tutorial for the Animation 2 badge, they watch each step as I create a simple hand-drawn animation of a bouncing ball, which is a skill that they will need to master if they are to complete the challenge. To demonstrate their understanding of each tutorial, students will complete tutorial projects—short, basic demonstrations of their skills. For Animation 2, the students must complete three short videos to showcase the three basic animation skills from the tutorials. This ensures that the students actually go through the tutorials (which they are sometimes tempted to skip) and allows them to practice isolated skills before using them in a more complex, creative undertaking.

Artifact Completion

Why do I call the result of all this work an artifact? To me an artifact is something made by a student that proves skills and knowledge of specific learning. It is the evidence that the student deserves the badge. Artifacts come in many formats—videos, photos, screencasts, audio recordings, and so on. Even for my students who publicly demonstrate their skills by performing, as with robotics or music, they still must

get video footage of that performance to be the artifact itself.
Here is a good example for a student earning their Music 2
badge by performing a cover of a song in front of people, in this
case hundreds of special ed teachers at a conference in Denver
(vimeo.com/158983395).

Once students have been instructed on and demonstrated the
necessary content and/or skills by completing the tutorials,
it's their turn to hone and demonstrate their own creativity
using the skills they have just learned (remember the Cut-the-
Rope game and "just in time" learning). At this point, they
receive the instructions and specifications for the artifact (the
evidence that they deserve the badge) that they will need to
create to demonstrate mastery of this skill. For example, here
is the challenge for Audio 1: "To earn this badge you need to
create a radio commercial (the artifact) under one minute long
about Operation Smile. Your commercial will be uploaded to
the school's YouTube channel to bring awareness to Operation
Smile. The best commercials will be featured on the school's
KJAG radio station." They receive a straightforward checklist
of artifact requirements that must be met. They also receive
a document from me to guide them through planning and
brainstorming. Then, using basic trial and error, returning
to tutorials, getting help from students who have mastered
the skill, or even asking the teacher, students work at their
own pace to complete the artifact. If this is an area where the
student already has a lot of prior knowledge or skill, they may
breeze through quickly. Some may have to practice hard or try
repeatedly before they can meet the standards.

Peer Review

Because the checklist is simple and straightforward, a lot can be expected of the self-review and peer-review process. If a student thinks they have a completed artifact, they can review the checklist themselves. Then, they are required to bring it to a peer, who will sign off on the artifact only if it truly meets all requirements. Students and peer reviewers are held accountable for the quality of artifacts that are submitted to the teacher.

The Teacher Feedback Cycle

Once the artifact has passed peer review, it is ready to be submitted to the teacher. The very name of this step denotes its difference from traditional grading. Students aren't submitting work for a one-shot final evaluation. Instead, they will be asked to improve their work if it doesn't meet the standards set forth. They don't fail the project—they simply have to fix it. There's no quibbling over percentages or letter grades—the artifact either meets the criteria, or it doesn't. If it doesn't, the project is simply returned to the student with feedback for improvement.

I use Google Classroom for the teacher feedback cycle (and the rest of the badge system administration, as I will discuss later). Assessment is simple, as I use a checklist similar to the one the student and peer reviewers used to make sure that the artifact is acceptable. The electronic submission platform of Google Classroom works well for my purposes, because students maintain access to the work they have turned in, and I can give them quick electronic feedback on what needs to be improved. Once they've made the necessary improvements, they simply resubmit their work. When I see that they've met all the criteria, the skill is recorded as complete, the badge is awarded, and the student can choose a new skill to work on.

Sharing, Helping, and Reflecting

As students turn in their artifacts, they also complete a short reflection about what and how they learned through the completion of this badge. They will be asked to record things like what problems they overcame or what they think stands out about their work. Once again, this step gives students responsibility for their own learning. They don't just turn it into me and wait to find out whether I think they've learned enough. Instead, they take ownership for their own learning processes. By analyzing their own learning, they continue to think critically and analytically by evaluating themselves and drawing larger conclusions from their experiences. Pausing and reflecting can help students solidify what they have learned and name the various skills they demonstrated.

After focusing on what they learned themselves, I also ask them to contribute to others' learning. A student who had earned a badge in any given skill is an expert of sorts in that area, so they are now qualified to assist others. Students are asked to spend a certain amount of time in this role when they have completed a badge. I added this step during the second year I tried the badge program. Once students had completed a badge, I required that they use 20 minutes of their time assisting someone else with the completion of that badge. I make it very clear that "helping" does not mean doing it for the other student, and clarify this by explaining that they should never touch the iPad or materials of the student they are helping. Not only does this solidify both the helped and the helper student's understanding of that skill, but it also builds those digital-age collaborative and problem-solving skills. Instead of immediately turning to the teacher when they hit a snag, students now have the resources I have prepared for them and the resources of one another. And remember, you don't truly know something new unless you can teach it to someone else.

Finally, the great work students have done needs to be shared. There are many places within the school and beyond that student work can be displayed, published, or demonstrated. Sometimes my students' work is shared via YouTube, sometimes it is on the school's website, and sometimes it is used in the school's promotional materials. Usually, students are aware of where their work might be shared as they create it, so they have the concept of a real audience to motivate them.

The Culminating Event

As mentioned earlier, all artifacts are designed to somehow contribute to a larger culminating event at the end of the unit or school year, and students know this as they work on them. It's very tempting to slack off on a paper that's just getting handed in to a teacher, but when students know their work is going on the school website or will be featured at the year-end event, a whole new standard emerges. More importantly, they are contributing to a larger cause.

In my program, for example, when students are working toward their Animation badge, their artifact is a promotional piece for the fundraiser. When they achieve their Digital Art badge, they are also creating work that will be sold at the fundraiser. They are doing their work not just for me, but for a real audience who will actually see their posters, watch their promos, and buy their art, and for the people who will benefit from the funds they raise. I have never seen students work more diligently than when they are motivated by both the prospect of a live performance and the responsibility of raising funds for a cause they care about. A culminating event might be any kind of performance, awareness campaign, fundraiser, demonstration, or fair. The important points are that it provides unity for the badge system, offers an authentic audience for student work, and gives students the opportunity to make a difference in the world.

CHAPTER FOUR

Creating Your Own Badge System

BY NOW, YOU'VE probably gathered that setting up a badge system requires a significant amount of upfront planning. It might sound overwhelming, but don't be intimidated. The effort is worth it, first, for the many benefits it brings the students. And, as a secondary benefit to the teacher, the intensive setup effort pays off when your unit or course essentially runs itself. Once you have designed the badge options, challenges, artifacts, and checklists, your students are off and running, and you transition into the roles of guide and accountability monitor. No Sunday night lesson plan struggles, no "What should I do with my fourth period class on Friday?" The initial planning pays great dividends for both students and teachers.

The last chapter went through how a student would move through a badge system chronologically. This one focuses on design from the teacher's side. In the following sections I share my eight steps for creating a badge system.

Step 1: Select the Subject

I do recommend starting small. I would not advise that you undertake a badge program in all of your classes or all of your subjects at once. When I was first experimenting with my idea, I used a small after-school club as my test group. This allowed me to identify problems and smooth out the wrinkles without having a negative impact on a large group of students. You might consider starting with a smaller class, a single non-core subject, an advanced or highly motivated group, or a unit or subject you know needs serious revamping anyway. For me, my subject was decided, as I am a technology teacher. I just had to decide which of my classes to start implementing it in. If you are an elementary teacher, you can choose any of the many subjects that you teach. If you are a specific subject area teacher, decide which of your courses or grade levels you'd like to try.

Step 2: Select the Project/Unit

The badge program that I designed spanned the entire year. I was able to incorporate all of the skills I wanted my students to master that year into my one multileveled badge unit. Yours could be a much more narrow unit with fewer skills, badges, or levels. For example, a third grade teacher may "badge-ify" the California Gold Rush unit as part of their history lesson, a high school biology teacher might use badges within their ecology unit, and a middle school English teacher might employ the badge system in a unit on dramatic writing.

To make your badge unit meaningful and engaging, the overarching theme should have real-world relevance. When I was creating my badge system on technology, I spent a lot of time thinking about what I really wanted my students to understand about technology. I determined that I wanted them to see technology as more than just an avenue for enter-tainment and convenience—I wanted them to realize that they could use technology to change the world. That might sound idealistic, but this is exactly the type of things students need to understand in order to grasp the importance of what they are studying. With this end in mind, I selected "Charity Fundraising" as the theme for my unit. All the skills my students learned would involve learning about and eventually raising funds for a selected charity. This theme was incredibly effective because I wasn't just telling students how they might be able to use technology to make the world better some-day—I was allowing them to do it right now. In *Literacy Is Not Enough*, Crockett, et. al. emphasize relevance, explaining that "For learning to occur, there must be relevance, not to the teacher, but to the learner. So clearly, the first component of 21st century learning is relevance" (Crockett, Jukes, & Churches, 2011).

Now, as a technology teacher, I had the luxury of being able to apply my subject area to virtually any theme I wanted. But within more content-focused subjects, real-world meaning can still be achieved. The subject might be history and the theme could be Ancient Greece.

Ideally, the unit, project, or lesson will be designed with a culminating event or project at the end. This is an opportunity for students to showcase the skills they have been learning in a meaningful way. As always, start small and work your way up. At my school's Kids Make a Difference Festival, for example we raise money for the charities that each of my grade levels have been focusing on throughout the year. This event is promoted by audio commercials, videos, and podcasts prepared as artifacts. Art that is created as artifacts can be sold. Films created as artifacts are shown as part of the film festival, and music composed or performed as artifacts provides entertainment. All the skills the students have been learning come together in a wonderful event that makes a difference.

It takes time and a lot of commitment to develop a large event like this. On a smaller scale, your unit or class could culminate in any event that gives students an authentic audience and, ideally, a chance to make a difference. This might be a simple classroom demonstration that parents are invited to, or any type of performance, exhibition, reading, display, fundraiser, fair, or community event. The biology students' Ecology Badge program might culminate with an environmental awareness drive or event of some sort. The drama unit in the English class might conclude with a performance night. The culminating event for the social studies class studying the California Gold Rush could be a live history tour, hosted by the class for students in another class. The scope and audience can vary, but having something "real" to build toward is valuable to student motivation.

Step 3: List Skills Needed for Success

While Step 2 presents a "big picture," Step 3 is where we get very practical. Starting with a brainstorm, list any and all of the skills that you believe students will need to be successful in the unit. Make sure to focus on skills—not knowledge. This is a critical point. Badges can be set up so that students acquire content knowledge as they pursue different skills, but badges should not be content based. For example, "Memorize the periodic table of elements" should not be one of the skills on your list. However, you might include a skill that requires knowledge of the periodic table to complete. In other words, students are acquiring content as needed to immediately perform a skill.

Skills can be discipline specific, but they could also include general academic, thinking, or social skills that are important to success in your discipline. Some of my additional skill ideas have been sparked by things students do that drive me crazy. For example, it irks me just a bit when I receive emails from students without a subject line, with no capital letters to be found in the entire email, or with the text of a paper pasted into the body of the email. So what did I do? I made all of these requirements part of the "email" skill. I also hate seeing students exclude one another in group settings. I could create a Leadership or Collaboration badge that would include skills like discussing, delegating, managing a meeting, or communication.

When I was finished with my skill list, it looked like the one shown in Figure 4.1. It included keyboarding, online safety, animation, email, podcasting, online research, presentations, filmmaking, academic papers, and digital portfolios.

A third grade teacher working on the California Gold Rush unit might include some of the following skills: map interpretation, reading primary sources, cause and effect relationships, research, and presentation. Notice that none of these skills are specific to the California Gold Rush, but all could certainly be applied to learning about the California Gold Rush. As students hone their research and map-reading skills, they will be encountering Gold-Rush related content.

SKILLS MY STUDENTS NEED
- online research
- online safety
- animation
- email
- presentations
- filmmaking
- keyboarding
- digital portolios
- file management
- iPad rules
- MacBook rules
- Google Apps
- Google Classroom

Figure 4.1 Skill list from brainstorming exercise

The English teacher creating a drama unit might list skills such as formatting (including stage directions, asides, lines, etc.), dynamic characterization, evaluating and critiquing, story structures, comparison and contrast, and subtext. They might also be reading and reacting to a Shakespeare play throughout the unit, and using that content to build these skills.

The biology teacher working on ecology might focus on the skills of structuring a scientific experiment, analyzing an ecosystem, recording scientific data, and writing a lab report.

Step 4: Sort Skills into Levels

Once you have a good list of skills, it's time to sort and categorize them. You will need to decide which skills are basic and foundational, and which might be higher-level challenges. At the lower level, I incorporated the absolute essential skills that I wanted every student to master. The highest-level skills are the "carrots" that I hoped would motivate students to press forward—the "fun" skills, such as 3D printing or filmmaking. The higher-level skills should also be skills that every student may not reach. They should provide substantial learning opportunities for students who do press on this far, but not be indispensable skills that a student will suffer for not having reached. This is where you can dream—you can include the skills that you may never get to when you're trying to keep the whole class at the same place.

Alternatively, you could develop a unit by rearranging steps 2 through 4. Instead of starting with a preselected unit, you could begin with the skill brainstorm, then begin grouping them, and then decide what type of content you will apply those skills to. For example, I actually started by listing all of the skills I wanted my students to learn first, and then I decided to organize them under the umbrella of the charity theme. A language arts teacher might also list and group all of the reading and writing skills they desire to teach, and then decide what overarching theme they will focus on as those skills are developed.

Step 5: Gather Skills into Badges

Back in step 4, you sorted your skills into levels. As you did, you may have found that some skills are very closely related, and that some skills are much more complex than others. As mentioned earlier, a single skill doesn't necessarily need to result in a badge. You could combine several skills that need to be mastered in order to earn a single badge. My Tech Basics badge, for example, requires students to know the file naming protocol that we use in our school, understand online safety, and be able to navigate Google Classroom.

Table 4.1 shows all of the badges and levels for my fourth grade technology class. You might notice that within my badges the same skill sometimes appears at multiple levels. You see that students can get both a Music 1 badge and a Music 2 badge, for example. Because I sorted my skills into levels before I created badges, I recognized that there are both foundational and higher-level music technology skills that I want my students to learn. At level 2, I wanted students to learn simple skills like using loops to create a song. I hoped that numerous students would attain these level 2 skills. However, I also had some more advanced music skills that I designated as level 4 skills, which included being able to perform in the iBand.

Table 4.1 Outline of Badges for Grade 4 Technology Class

LEVEL 1 (ROOKIE) BADGES

Badge	Skills Required
Tech Basics*	online safety, technology rules, file naming
Email*	subject lines, reply, forward, attach files, delete, and etiquette
Digital Student*	online research, Google Classroom, formatting documents and presentations
Digital Portfolio*	adding entries, organizing, and commenting
Keyboarding*	typing more than 20 words per minute

LEVEL 2 (EXPLORER) BADGES

Badge	Skills Required
Music 1	Create an original song in GarageBand using loops to serve as the background music for a festival promotional video
Animation 2*	Create a hand-drawn animation to bring awareness to the charity and to support the festival.
Video 1	Create a 30-second commercial to bring awareness to the charity and to support the festival.
Art 2	Create an original digital painting that is connected to the charity and that will be sold at the art auction during the festival.

LEVEL 3 (APPRENTICE) BADGES

Badge	Skills Required
Animation 3	Create a 3-minute clay animation/Legomation to teach about Kiva.org.
Audio 2*	Create a 5-minute podcast about Kiva.org in the style of NPR storytelling.
Video 2	Create a 7-minute documentary about Kiva.org.
Music 2	Perform a cover of a song using just chords to bring awareness and support for Kiva.org.

*Required badge; all others are optional

This is something that you can consider as well, and it is also why dividing skills into levels before badges is so important. You might want students to learn skills that seem similar topically, but actually vary widely in complexity. For example, the third grade teacher designing a California Gold Rush system might have a Maps 1 badge in level 1, where students demonstrate basic map reading skills. Then, up in level 3, Maps 2 might involve creating or designing maps. If this teacher bunched all the map skills together by topic, without considering the different levels of the skills, the Maps badge would be a daunting one, and the basic essential skills would be lumped together with more difficult ones. So don't forget about the possibility of offering multiple badges at different levels to allow students to build skills progressively and then further pursue those they found interesting later.

As you design badges and levels, you will also have to think about which badges will be required and which will be optional. I require all students to earn all level 1 badges before moving on. Then, at level 2, they are able to choose two of the four badges to complete the level. Every student will not earn every badge, so be strategic about which skills are must-learn and which skills could be optional.

Step 6: Design the Artifact for Each Badge

How will I know that the student has mastered each skill? This is the driving question of step 6. If I want my students to be proficient animators, what do they need to show me? I decided that to earn an Animation 1 badge, students would have to create a 60-second animated video that met certain criteria. An English teacher who wants his students to demonstrate the skill of critiquing a drama has many options for what type of artifact he will accept. He could ask for a piece of writing that meets certain specifications, a video or podcast review featuring one or more students, à la Siskel and Ebert, or a submission to a class blog where each student submits an evaluation of a different work.

As you are deciding what the artifact will be, you can also develop right then a straightforward checklist of criteria that this artifact must meet (an example checklist from my Audio 1 badge is shown in Figure 4.2). Remember that successfully completing an artifact is a yes-or-no question—you aren't creating a complicated rubric with gradations of success. This type of evaluative tool does *not*, however, mean that you are grading at a low standard. In fact, I would encourage you to attach a very high standard to each artifact. Students have time and opportunity to try as long and as often as needed to successfully complete the artifact, and this single project is going to be evidence of their mastery of a skill.

To earn this badge you must have done the following:

You have created a radio commercial...

☐ It is less than 60 seconds.

☐ It has music in the background at the appropriate volume.

☐ The speaker is clear and easy to understand.

☐ You state your first name and what class you are in.

☐ You finish your commercial with "Let's show the world that MET students can make a difference."

☐ You tell listeners to support Operation Smile by attending the upcoming Kids Can Make a Difference Festival.

Figure 4.2 Example Checklist for Audio 1 Badge

I have been absolutely astounded by the quality of work I have seen in my students' artifacts. Once they realized that I actually expected them to complete every part as instructed (no sliding through with several missing pieces and a 70%), students rose to the occasion. And, once I began collecting and sharing examples from past students, students believed even more strongly that they could succeed in what was being asked of them.

Checkpoint 1: Do the Artifacts Connect to the Unit Theme?

Keeping in mind the idea of relevance, the system is far more effective if these artifacts can be somehow connected to both the unit theme and the students' real world. If you are teaching an academic subject, you have likely already considered the relevance of the artifact to the unit's topic. All of your artifacts in the drama unit are likely going to have some relevance to drama, whether they are performances, critiques, analyses, or original writing. Those who teach a more skill-based class, such as technology, mathematics, art, music, or physical education, might have to put a little more thought into unifying their artifacts thematically.

While you consider the thematic unity of the artifacts, this is also a good time to consider how each one could contribute to a culminating event. Anything that puts student work in front of an authentic audience immediately adds meaning. Performance and publication, whether electronic or in print, for parents, the school, the community or the world, will motivate students.

In the case of the culminating event for my course, the Kids Make a Difference fundraiser, almost every artifact the students will create has some connection to this event. Students' completed digital painting artifacts are printed and sold as part of the fundraiser. Students' Animation artifacts are promotional videos, sharing facts about the charity and persuading people to attend the event. Music and film production artifacts provide the entertainment at the festival, and even video game creation depicts the problems being overcome by the charity. To make every artifact worthwhile, consider what role it could play in promoting, preparing for, or contributing to the culminating event.

Checkpoint 2: Do the Artifacts Require Higher-Order Thinking Skills?

No matter where or what grade level you teach, you are probably familiar with the levels of critical thinking, or Bloom's taxonomy. You may have seen them illustrated on a pyramid, a wheel, a list, or a ladder, filled with action verbs that depict what students might be asked to do at each level. There has been, rightly, a push to move away from the lower level skills that focus on rote memorization and recitation, such as reciting, recalling, naming, or listing. These can be important foundational skills, but once again, we live in a world where gaining information isn't the challenge. We want students to be able to do things, make things, discover things, and create things. These activities require the higher-order skills of applying, adapting, generating, synthesizing, and designing.

As we design artifacts, then, we must make sure we are not just asking for a very fancy low-level project. For my Design badge, the artifact was a T-shirt that promoted the charity being studied. However, I realized that I had designed this artifact in such a way that students were merely "filling in the blanks." The T-shirts were turning out great, but the students weren't strategizing or analyzing the impact of their design choices as they worked. I had created an artifact challenge that required only low-level critical thinking. I then redesigned the badge in such a way that students learned general design principles, but had much more freedom to create something based on those principles, rather than just following step-by-step instructions. They had to incorporate their understanding of color, contrast, readability, and other design principles to achieve a desired effect. Now, they were thinking at a higher level.

A student could spend hours creating a Lego model of a plant cell. It might turn out beautifully, but the student has shown only the most rote, basic understanding of a cell's parts. They could have stared at a labeled picture the whole time, reproduced it faithfully, and still learned very little content and no useful skills aside from Lego engineering. They may have learned the names of a couple of cell parts, if we're lucky, but they have demonstrated no understanding of the way a cell works, and they won't walk away from completing that artifact having learned any useful skill. Instead, a student could create a narrated animation of a cell's function, or prepare thoroughly to interview an expert about how a cell works. These students have interacted more meaningfully with the subject matter and walked away with transferable skills because they are using higher-level critical thinking skills.

Step 7: List/Gather Resources Needed

This is fairly self-explanatory, but it is important to address early in the process. It can often take time to gain approval for new supplies, order them, or even raise funds for them if needed. Look at every skill in every badge and list everything you may need—from pens and markers to internet connections to computers to software or apps. Remember that not every student will be working on the same stage of the same badge at once, but it is likely that multiple students will need the same supplies at some point. However, if supplies are short, a reservation/ rotation system can be established, and students can be asked to make progress on another skill or badge while they wait. You do, however, want to make sure that all necessary supplies can be acquired to avoid having to change something midway through.

Now you've established the scope of your unit, brainstormed skills, established badges, and even thought about what the ultimate artifact might be at the end of each badge. Now, you can turn your attention to designing each individual badge.

Step 8: Select Learning Management and Badging Systems

Since I use Google Classroom for my learning management system (LMS), I need to use a separate system to track the badges so I know who has earned what. For the first few years I just used my old-school grade book; now I use Credly. Services like Edmodo and Schoology have both the LMS and the badge tracking systems built together.

Once you have your LMS and badging systems selected, it is now just a matter of building the classes (levels) and the assignments (badges). Then you just simply upload or link files to each assignment.

CHAPTER FIVE

Creating Individual Badge Challenges

WE'VE WORKED OUR WAY back to the very beginning of earning a badge now. But before the students jump into whatever tutorials you selected or created in step 8, the students will need to know why they are learning these skills and how they will be expected to use them.

Part 1: Introduction and Challenge Video

I have a lot of fun with this element of the plan. Even though it's a relatively minor part of the badge system, it really does a lot to set the tone and generate excitement. My badge challenge video is usually just a simple one-take video of myself giving an overview of the skills, an explanation of why the skills are important, and an idea of what they'll be asked to do as the final challenge. I keep the tone enthusiastic and upbeat, almost daring them to do something great.

In my challenge video for animation, for example, I mention examples that students are familiar with (such as Disney films and Pixar films and shorts) and explain that the techniques they will be learning are the very basic foundations that these animators use. I also ask that if they become famous animators, they remember my class, and come back and treat me to dinner or something. They have now seen that their learning has real-world applications and that I have high expectations of them. Every time I teach a new skill, I believe that there is a real possibility that it could become a lifelong passion for one or more of my students.

Before they get going on the badge, I then like to give them a few questions to think about. For example, here are the questions from the Level 2, Music 1 badge:

1. **Factual.** How do you convert the length of your video from seconds to bars?

2. **Conceptual.** How can music change someone's mood?

3. **Debatable.** What style of music is best suited to promote this year's festival?

These should get the gears turning, and later on they will answer these questions during their final reflection piece.

Part 2: Student Example

I was hesitant to use student examples as first, as I was afraid it would stifle student creativity—wouldn't all of them just copy the example? However, I have found that the advantages of using student examples outweigh this concern. First, examples provide more clarity in what is expected than 10 pages of requirements and directions could. I show work that I deem to be "high quality," and students therefore understand that the bar is high. Second, students are inspired and infused with confidence when they see excellent work that their peers (or, better yet, students younger than them!) have done. Finally, many students don't see the example as something to copy— they see it as something to beat.

For my animation badge, I show them short animations of a bouncing ball, a lighthouse with a light circling around a stationary pillar, and an example of wiggle art. The students don't yet know how they will accomplish these techniques, but they are excited by the end result and motivated to learn the skills they will need to achieve this badge.

Part 3: What You Need

You already listed the supplies needed for the entire unit, but within the introduction of each badge, students should be introduced to the supplies they will need for that particular badge. That way, they know what they need to bring to class and what materials they need to reserve or borrow in the near future.

Part 4: Gather and/or Create Tutorials

We're working backward a bit, as you've likely noticed. We started with the overarching theme and the final, major event that the whole unit builds toward, envisioned the world-changing skills you want your students to emerge with, and selected the artifacts that will demonstrate those skills. But there's still a large piece missing. How will students actually learn the skills and content that you want them to learn? They need to be shown how to do what they are being asked to do.

One option for this stage is to direct students to resources that already exist. There are numerous excellent educational videos and lectures available on YouTube, Kahn Academy, BrainPOP, Atomic Learning, and iTunes U. Some teachers who have implemented the flipped classroom system are willing to share or sell the videos they have created. You may be able to find a video or podcast that walks students through the skills you would like them to learn. There may be articles with great illustrations or graphics. If you need to teach your third graders the basics of map reading, a YouTube search turns up several videos—some in song—that walk students through the basics. If one tutorial doesn't explain everything, students can be directed to more than one resource, too.

This might initially strike some teachers as "lazy," since they themselves aren't doing the explanation. But your value as a teacher doesn't lie in knowing things that no one else knows. Instead, see yourself as a guide who is helping students find and use the excellent resources that will always be at their disposal. Many teachers like feeling "needed" by their students, but a truly great teacher prepares her students to succeed on their own—long after they are out of her classroom. A classroom lecture is a one-shot opportunity. If a student is absent, distracted, tired, confused, or bored during those crucial 10 minutes (and let's not speculate on what percentage that may be), they will miss the information and be lost moving forward. If they are, instead, connected to resources they can access independently, they can revisit the information as often and as slowly as they need to.

However, you can still function as one of those resources, and you can create tutorials, too. You can use the video function on a phone or a tablet to shoot video of varying complexity, walking students through the skills you would like them to learn. I often set my iPad up to record an over-the-shoulder shot of me performing a skill on another iPad as I talk through it, step by step. You could also employ any of the many fantastic apps, such as Explain Everything, that allow you to record your writing and speaking simultaneously, so that students can follow your explanation as you solve an equation, draw a diagram, or sketch a map. If you have slide presentations that you had previously designed, you may be able to make use of them by pairing them with recorded narration, allowing students to learn from them independently.

In my animation tutorial, I set up the iPad camera behind me, tapped on the app that the students would need to use, and simply talked through and demonstrated the process for creating an animated bouncing ball in that app. They can see how I interact with the features of the app, and I explain why and how I do each step.

Sometimes it takes me a couple of takes to get the tutorial smooth and clear, but once I've gotten a good video, I have a resource I can use for years. I have found that making videos of short lessons like this one really distills my teaching technique and forces me to stay focused on the essentials. Since it isn't a live lecture, I can't count on student questions to prompt me to clarify unclear places or add in information that I skipped.

Whether you create the resource yourself or direct your students to other sources, you are giving them the tools to take learning into their own hands during this phase of the system. Of course, you can still be available to answer questions and check in with students—I do so very frequently. However, if students ask for something that was already covered in one of the resources, direct them back to it. Students sometimes see asking the teacher as the easier option, whether the alternative is opening a book or replaying a video. Since part of the goal is to create more independent and self-directed students, you need to be clear that your role is to supplement and expand on the tutorials—not replace them.

After you have created or located the tutorials you plan to use, think about how students could demonstrate the basic skills contained in them. Before students move on to the larger arti- fact, I like to incorporate a checkpoint I call a tutorial project to ensure that they have watched the tutorials and practiced the skills enough to be able to successfully complete the final artifact. After the Animation II tutorial, students need to show me two short videos: one of a bouncing ball, indicating their ability to animate motion, and one of a rotating lighthouse, to demonstrate their ability to combine a still object and a moving object. Once they have demonstrated these skills, they are ready to attempt to earn their badge by creating the arti- fact (that was the commercial discussed earlier). Decide how students can demonstrate the skill they have just learned in a simple and basic manner before they move on to the artifact, which is usually more creative and requires higher-level thinking.

Here is a word of caution. Some students are impatient and like to skip the tutorials—they want to dive right in without any skills. They are reluctant to go through instructions step by step. They become restless, and they can't wait to tinker around and try something new with the right tools in hand. This is why my students must show me the results from the tutorial before they can go on to working on the actual challenge. If you allow students to skip the tutorial, you will get inundated with questions that could have been answered if they had just completed the tutorial project. But just because they have the tool does not mean they know how to use it. Therefore, you need to put in a comprehensive tutorial and make sure the students to go through it.

The tutorials are the key to give students the essential skills to create amazing outputs. They are essential for skill building. Therefore, before I run the badge program, I tell the students to follow the tutorials exactly as possible without any deviations. Essentially, this is the stage where they need to hold their creative horses. First gain the skills—then they can use those skills to unleash their creativity for the final artifact. This is one of the reasons that I require students to turn in the more basic tutorial projects before moving on to the artifacts.

When I first started the program, I didn't initially require these types of projects. I had really committed to the "at your own pace" idea and wanted students to be able to fly through unrestricted if they were already competent at a skill. But, I found that some students thought they were already proficient—but then had a million questions about how to do the challenge. They were skipping the tutorials, trying to complete the artifacts without acquiring the skills they needed, and then asking me for instruction that the tutorials would have provided. So, I instituted mandatory tutorial projects to ensure that the students were actually taking part in the tutorials.

Students need to be patient with the tutorial process. The tutorials serve as a guided discovery for them, where they will discover great things about animation as long as they stay on the guided path. Once they have the skills, they can leave this path to create anything they deem is better.

Part 5: Challenge Project (Artifact)

Artifacts were discussed in the last chapter to some extent. I do encourage thinking about artifacts as a part of the larger system design for a few reasons. First, you can make sure you are developing a well-rounded variety of artifacts. Second, you can make sure that each badge you are choosing to award can be well represented by an artifact that ties into the theme.

As you know, once students have gone through the tutorials as much as needed and done the necessary practice to master some of the basic skills, they will be ready to attempt the challenge project. This will be the "artifact" that will demonstrate skill mastery and tie in to the unit's overall theme.

The challenge project for my Animation 2 badge is to create an animated video about Kiva that will be used to teach the younger students about what the charity does. Students use their newfound animation skills to research and promote a cause that is important to them, and then spread awareness of that cause through their animated video.

This is a good example of a place where students are motivated to encounter and understand content in the context of performing a skill. A student could not successfully complete this project without having a strong understanding of the facts she was presenting in her animation. Thus, we have motivated (or tricked) a student into pursuing content because they have an immediate need to use them in the demonstration of their skill.

This is also a good example of a challenge project that sets the bar high. The video has to reach a certain length, and it has to include a certain number of frames, a certain number of facts, and demonstration of certain techniques. A student who meets all of the criteria has certainly shown mastery of basic animation skills and has already applied those skills to a project of real-world relevance.

Part 6: Peer-Reviewed Checklist

How will students know if they've met the high standard that I've mentioned several times? The peer review checklist helps make students accountable for the quality of their own and others' work. Grading should never have been a mysterious roll of the dice where students turn in a project and cross their fingers, with no idea whether they'll get a D or a B. In the same way, students should never have to submit a completed project and wonder whether or not it will be approved. They have the checklist I will use to evaluate it, and they are required to have a peer go through that checklist with them.

I can imagine that some teachers have had negative experiences with peer reviewing, where students are afraid to criticize one another or just don't make the effort to carefully critique their classmates' work. First, the simplicity and objectivity of the checklist should make the task of peer reviewing more manageable and straightforward. Second, I emphasize the responsibility and importance of this step, and I follow up with both the creator and the reviewer of a product when peer reviewing is done poorly.

This is an important step—first, because it pushes students to make sure their work is done well before submitting it, lessening the time it might spend in the teacher feedback cycle. Second, it builds collaboration and communication skills that are essential in school and beyond. Reviewers must learn to be tactful yet honest, and students having their work reviewed learn the value of a second set of eyes.

Part 7: Share with the World

This might seem like an extra or optional step at the end, and it might be one that you are tempted to skip for various reasons. Maybe you are uncertain of what platforms to use or how to use them. Maybe you have been inundated with warnings about student privacy and online safety. Please don't avoid or skip this step for those reasons. Having an audience beyond the teacher drives students to work harder and complete better work than I have ever seen before. Work can be shared via a classroom or school social media account, website, or YouTube channel. Let students know the venue for sharing when they first receive the challenge so that they are working with a larger audience in mind.

I sometimes hear concerns about this step, with people citing the dangers of putting student work online. Yes, there is some danger anytime a young student is online, but the truth is the web is just so different than it was even a few years ago when most of our online "rules" were developed. We made rules like "never put anything online" before sites like Facebook and Instagram even existed. The reality is that everything is online, privacy is being redefined, and the thought of our kids not learning how to responsibly post content online has turned out to be the scariest part of all. Our students are already posting

Figure 5.1 Sharing their projects with a larger audience can motivate students.

silly videos, event invitations, and pictures of what they ate for dinner. Why not teach them to responsibly post things that make them look good, like high-quality academic work?

Part 8: Reflection

In the penultimate step, prepare reflection questions for students to complete as they finish and turn in their artifact. I have a few standard questions that I generally adapt to each unit, such as the questions for the Claymation badge below:

1. How much did you know about clay animation before you started?

2. What problems did you encounter while you were working on this piece? How did you solve them?

3. What was especially satisfying to you about either the process or the finished product?

4. What do your classmates particularly notice about your piece when they look at it?

Keep questions somewhat open-ended, but not too broad to inspire thoughtful reflection. I have found that questions with stems like the ones just listed help guide students toward specific facets of learning to focus on, as opposed to questions such as "What did you learn?" or "What did you do well?"

Finally: Launch, Revise, and Enjoy

With challenges made, tutorials and resources lined up, artifacts with checklists planned, badges and skills determined, and a motivating theme and final project, you have all the makings of success. Things are guaranteed to go perfectly after all of this preparation, right? Unfortunately, there will be some growing pains associated with such a significant transition. For one thing, you might face questions, and maybe even doubts, from a variety of sources—your students, their parents, your co-workers, or your administration. And, you will probably discover some hiccups, shall we say, in the program yourself. Perhaps you'll find that students bottleneck at a certain skill, and you are short on resources. Perhaps learning some skills will take far longer than you anticipated, and others far less time. And of course, there's always the discovery that you've left an essential requirement off of the artifact checklist, leaving a major loophole that students happily exploit. Whatever the case may be, remember that you're learning, too. You are creating, designing, and experimenting, just as you'll be asking your students to do. What a great opportunity to show them that even you have to go back to the drawing board at times!

However, despite the need for some revision, I can almost guarantee that the implementation of the badge program will bring joy to your teaching like never before. I wish I could transport each reader to my classroom in Panama (and not just for the weather). If you could feel the buzz of excitement and hear the questioning, collaborating, and problem solving that takes place on a daily basis, you wouldn't be able to resist giving the badge system a try.

CHAPTER SIX

Implementation Tips

SINCE I HAVE BEEN USING the system for several years now, I have helpfully made a number of mistakes for you and can report back to help you avoid them. Don't worry—you'll still get to make mistakes of your own. They just won't be the same ones I made. I have also seen a number of elements that do work and are important to include.

Managing the Badge System

On the logistical side of things, you must find a central place where students can find the badge-related information: challenge videos, tutorials, checklists, and other resources. This could, and probably should, be the same place where students can submit their work. Because the system is often self-paced, and students need to be able to access it independently, there needs to be a single, organized interface that students can navigate with ease. Students also need to be able to access the information independently so that they can progress on their own schedule, including outside of school. There are different places to do so, starting from the internal server at your school as a part of a class website. For me, the school's server was not a viable option, so I had to look elsewhere.

I ultimately found that Google Classroom was the best interface for my situation. I have had great feedback from teachers using Edmodo and Schoology with equal success. Regardless of the LMS, students need a single "command center" for everything related to the class and the badges. In Google Classroom all of the videos, documents, resources, and instructions can be displayed for each of my classes. Once students are signed in as a member of a certain class, they can see all of the available the badges at a glance. Then, when they click on any of the badges, they can immediately access all resources and information for that badge. They can see deadlines, if applicable, and they can turn in their work electronically.

From my end, I can easily track the progress of each student and communicate with students quickly, and I'll never lose an assignment. I can very quickly see how many students have completed each step for each badge. I can also give them quick feedback electronically.

Introducing the Badge System

Start Small with a Pilot Program

When I started the concept of badges, I took it small with five students. I got their interest and ran a pilot for one year after school hours. It helped me because I could focus my energy on only five kids to get the right results. The five students would flaunt their badges on their backpacks, and this made other students curious and want the badges too ... badly!

By running a pilot, I had hit two birds with one stone. I got enough student examples to scale up my badge program. I had evidence of success, which helped me gain a sign-off from the principal, parents, and others, as you will see later. A pilot program also gives you an opportunity to gauge gaps and bugs and fix them before you scale up to the complete class or school.

Getting Buy-In from Your Stakeholders

Identifying stakeholders is a common practice while starting any project, but building a badge system touches life in the school as well as outside of the school. More importantly, a successful badge program also creates an association across different institutions. The most prominent stakeholders include your school principal, the students, and their parents.

Principal

As I mentioned earlier in the book, running a pilot program is essential for a successful badge program. It allows me to create a business case, which I can present to the school principal to make them aware of the initiative. It clearly explains the idea of badges, and, more importantly, its success, and its potential to be a schoolwide success. Since my badges were not replacing the traditional letter grades that come from the usual quizzes and tests, it was easy for her to see that badges were an excellent way to track skills—something that is usually not done. She recognized the badge system as a way to monitor and communicate student progress. In addition to, or instead of, a letter grade, the school can give parents and the community a much more concrete picture of what their student is actually learning. Instead of quibbling over why a student got a B instead of an A, the focus could shift to what skills a student has accomplished. It should be noted that after the first year, my badges did replace the letter grades. However, to make reports cards easy to understand, we came up with a formula for what badges would equal what grade. For example to get an A, a student would have to complete at least one level 4 badge.

It's important to make sure principals, department heads, and other administrators are brought into your plans early on and that communication is strong. Explaining it to these key stakeholders early on generates ownership and commitment. Ask for their feedback early and often, and clear any resistance that may arise in the process.

Parents

I have never faced any issue in getting buy-in from parents. In my situation, parents who had seen their children do nothing but waste time with their technology were thrilled at the prospect of their children using technology in a more productive way. They would much rather their kids used their iPad to create an original promotional video than to mindlessly watch silly YouTube videos. Moreover, they appreciate the fact that badges give a feeling of self-responsibility to the students, and they can build on their skills at their own pace. Many parents have shared their child's frustration at feeling either left behind or held back by the pace of a traditional classroom, so this can be a major selling point for parents.

In the same way as school administrators appreciate being included early on, parents do as well. A shift to a badge system is a fairly significant change to the way their child will experience school, and it's best that they hear from you what the purpose and advantages of this change are. This might include a presentation at an open house or "back to school" event, letters, emails, or other communications.

Students

Now, here is the hardest part. How do you get your students' buy-in on the badge program? Well, to be honest, you will struggle. So of course, the first 45 days will be the toughest for you. Students want the badges, but they do not want to do what it takes to get them. In my experience of teaching third, fourth, and fifth grade, students will look to the teacher for content and directions, and sometimes get frustrated when they are directed elsewhere. This isn't surprising, though, since traditional teaching often programs them to see the teacher as the center of any educational experience. They aren't used to taking charge of their own learning.

A badges program is different. It is all about independent learning. At first, they may hate it, especially when they do not get any instructions from you. The fact that students have to go back, visit the Google Classroom, and watch a video does not really sink in at first. As a teacher, you have to take responsibility and ensure that the kids learn independently. It may be challenging for the first several days, but gradually they will get used to it. Students will need to see that you are not abandoning them to videos, but that you are simply taking on a different role. And as they get used to it, they begin to love the independence and accomplishment they feel as they move to the driver's seat of their education.

Students also need to see the broader value of the program, especially if they are older. They need to understand what's in it for them. The philosophy behind the program can be explained to some extent, but seeing these ideals in action may be what it takes to win some students over. With every badge, be sure to both explain the real-world importance of the skill and provide an opportunity for them to use it in a meaningful way.

By the time I launched my badge program classroom-wide, students had seen the pilot program students' badges and were very curious. Before I even explained the system, they wanted badges of their own. Do not underestimate the design elements of the badges. Attractive badges can play a big role in building excitement and appealing to students. Badges should include a clear, identifiable image so that a viewer can immediately relate to the skill the badge is trying to portray. You will need to think about the visual appeal vis-à-vis the size, the appearance, whether it can be shared digitally, and so on. Don't overlook the step of creating exciting-looking badges that will pique students' curiosity and become a source of pride in your classroom.

Managing students' experience with the program is a key factor in gaining student buy-in. Word of mouth travels quickly, and good student experiences carry a lot of weight. Positive buzz from my pilot program provided a great starting point for my classroom-wide launch. Unfortunately, a bad student experience can ruin the most carefully designed badge system. For example, a clunky platform that hosts the badge program can hinder the understanding, learning, and sharing of badges. This leaves the students frustrated when trying to navigate the website. If students are trying and failing to access class materials, their enthusiasm will quickly wane. If one of the artifacts wasn't properly tested and turns out to be impossible to achieve as described, students will view future challenges dubiously.

My final word of advice to achieve buy-in from all stakeholders is to design the system based on the needs of your school and your students. Never design a system that is based on the values and assumptions of a different school. The badges system is flexible and customizable, so there is never one right way to implement it. That's why adopting someone else's whole program in its entirety probably wouldn't work. Depending on location, size, finances, demographics, and more, different students will have different needs. So don't leave your own expertise and understanding of your students at the door when you begin implementing the badge system.

CHAPTER SEVEN

A Word About Technology

AS I SAID EARLIER, a badge program does not necessarily require a technology-heavy classroom, but I do want to emphasize the important role technology can play in a badge program. An increasing number of teachers are working in environments where students are using school-issued devices at all times, and many others have ample access to at least a few devices. In fact, even if funds could be raised for a couple of tablets per classroom, you can incorporate at least some technology into your badge program.

I encourage you to incorporate some technology skills that are relevant in your discipline into your badge program. Technology does not, by itself, provide the needed transformation to 21st-century education. However, it can play a significant part in seeing education in a new way.

Using Technology in the Badge System

I use technology heavily in the way I administer my badge program. I can't imagine how I would keep track of the barrage of incoming work from each student (videos, photos, documents) without Google Classroom. For example, it allows me to perform several of the key tasks for my system's organization, including displaying the different badge challenges; housing all of the challenge videos, tutorials, student examples, and other resources students need; accepting students' completed projects; providing electronic feedback to students; and tracking students' progress and badges earned. A web-based platform has been the hub for my badge program for as long as I have run it, and it has worked extremely well. Students need to be able to access all the class resources anytime and anywhere.

You've probably gathered that videos play a big part in my system. Could I run a badge system without videos? Probably. But I wouldn't want to. Videos engage students and incorporate examples and explanation, unlike the written word alone, and students can return to them time and time again. The good news is that making and posting videos does not require vast technological knowledge. Today, most people have the ability to record and post videos even on their cell phones. If you can find the camera icon on an iPad, you can shoot a video.

TIP: Organizing Files in a Badge System

When I am working on a new badge, I begin by creating five folders.

1. **Instructions.** This is where I put tutorial videos, links to online lessons, etc.

2. **Student Work.** This is where I put the checklists, brainstorming, planning, and reflection documents. Any documents that students will fill out.

3. **Student Examples.** I put examples of best practices from the previous years. Every time I come across an amazing artifact, I make sure to put it in here so the students next year will see it as the student example.

4. **Support Files.** Any other files that students might need; audio files, photos, etc.

5. **Photos.** I like to have students take photos as they work on each badge. They then submit the best ones to me, and I collect them in this folder. I use these photos to show others what it looks like for students to work on a badge.

Second, I believe it is essential for students to understand how technology can be used productively in each discipline. Many teachers shy away from technology, thinking that students are far more knowledgeable than they are. Today's students are certainly technology natives and have grown up among touch screens and tweets. However, students do not necessarily absorb academic technology skills while they use their devices for texting, Snapchatting, Instagramming, and, of course, game playing. I've found that students don't know how to use a number of the apps on their school-issued iPads because they've never been taught or asked to use them. I've known of high school students who don't know how to insert page numbers on documents or attach documents to emails because teachers have assumed those were things they already knew how to do, and no one ever taught it. Smartphones and apps are so intuitive and user friendly that our apparently tech-savvy students might actually be puzzled by procedures that require more than a tap and a swipe.

The point is, students need instruction on how technology can be used to chart data, create maps, illustrate mathematical processes, create multimedia presentations, and collaborate with classmates. They need to realize that technology has purposes far greater than entertainment—that it can, in fact, be used to change the world for the better. But most of them won't realize it by accident. If we don't show them, we are missing a major opportunity to prepare our students for life beyond our classroom.

Technology and Student Potential

I have also found that technology is an area in which, for some reason, teachers tend to accept subpar work. It might be because they themselves are uncertain about how to troubleshoot or use an app to its potential. It may be because they still see technology as an add-on, or as something they incorporate just to make a project more fun or engaging. I argue, though, that students should be held to just as high a standard in technology as they are in other academic skills. Of course, work should be age appropriate, but we need to ask students for excellent work in the technology arena.

This point was driven home to me when I came across the work of Dr. Tim Tyson, who, at the time, was the principal of the Mabry Middle School in Marietta, GA. As I was researching podcasting, I encountered his school's website (www.MabryOnline.org) where he still keeps his podcasts archived. What happened next changed me as a teacher for the rest of my life.

While on the Mabry website, I saw a link to their 2007 film festival. I clicked the link, and soon I was watching the film work his middle school students had done. I was blown away, to say the least. I had never seen this type of quality work from college students, let alone middle schoolers.

Within days I was on the phone to Dr. Tyson asking him all sorts of questions, starting with the biggest one I had: "Who really made those movies?" He told me in a matter-of-fact tone that his students had. I told him I didn't believe him. He laughed and explained to me that he gets that a lot. He assured me that they had a high expectation when it came to the tech projects that the students make at his middle school. At Mabry they do not allow their students to do sloppy film work. Instead, they needed to follow a quality checklist with areas like sound, lighting, and so on.

It was as if he flipped a switch inside of me. I had no idea that young students were capable of such great work. Here I was, an elementary tech teacher, and now I knew what I wanted my students to do. I wanted them to make such incredible technology projects that people would be calling me someday asking who really made them. I wanted people to say, "There is no way a third grader took that great photo" or ask, "How many grownups helped make that movie about the Civil War?" What I wanted were unbelievable tech projects for my elementary students. I wanted to push my students to do great work with technology, not just mediocre work. I wanted them to do projects that they could put in their digital portfolios and say with pride years later, "Yeah. I made this movie when I was in elementary school—pretty cool, huh?"

To get better technology projects, we need to demand better technology projects. No different than what we expect from student projects in reading, writing, math, science, geography, and so on. We must demand the very best technology projects from our students. The employment-world they will soon be entering into will expect nothing less than this.

Lack of Funds for Technology

You may be interested in incorporating more technology, but find that money is a barrier. This is not an uncommon experience. Readers may say, "I like what Brad is doing with his students, but he comes from a brand-new school in an affluent neighborhood. We just don't have those kinds of resources." I really do get this kind of thinking, and there is some truth to it, but let me explain how things really work at my "rich" school.

It is true that my school is brand new, and that in my school we have less than 1% free and reduced lunch students (which I think is a nice way of saying that we have none). But the reality is that the only tech we had in the school when it opened was the two computer labs of 28 PCs each. Nothing else. No cameras, no podcasting studio, nothing. So I had to go "begging for bucks" just like anyone else.

The first wall I hit was that with my lack of a free and reduced rate I was not eligible for 95% of the funding programs out there, and for good reasons, I guess. But at the time it did not seem very fair. At the middle school where my wife was the principal, she raised over $1.3 million in less than three years with her free and reduced rate of 78%. This was due in part to the sheer number of grants that she was eligible to apply for.

I did apply for every grant and program that we were eligible for, but to get movie making started in my school, I turned to my PTO. I had just finished making a movie with my students using a simple Flip video camera, so I asked them for $1200 to purchase an HD video camera and a tripod so that I could start to make more movies with the kids. Six months and several spectacular student videos later, I asked for enough money to buy seven Flip video cameras, which they gladly gave me after the positive feedback they got from the students and parents about the previous movie projects. We now had filmmaking at our school.

My point is this: You have to earn your money, and you earn it by doing ambitious projects with what you already have. A few years ago we celebrated the 500th episode of our school podcast. This episode was recorded in our beautiful studio full of high-tech equipment, but the first 200 episodes were recorded with $8 microphones from Walmart and a refurbished computer. This past summer we were awarded a grant with enough money to fill our news studio with amazing equipment—because we earned it. We proved to those who hold the purse strings that it was a good investment.

CHAPTER EIGHT

Success Stories

I DON'T JUST BELIEVE in my badge system by virtue of the fact that I thought of it. (I've had plenty of ideas that have not fared nearly as well.) What has convinced me that I am on the right track is the overwhelming success and attitude change I have seen in the students who learn in this way. I don't want to pat myself on the back or brag—I just want to give you a small taste of the great things that are happening in badge system classrooms and, I hope, inspire you to give it a try.

In general, I, along with the other brave teachers who have attempted this system, have noticed increased student engagement and buy-in, fewer classroom management issues, and much higher quality work that we have received in the past. Students are taking ownership of their learning—so much so, that they are voluntarily working toward badges on their own time. Maybe most importantly, they are finding tremendous fulfillment in realizing that the skills they learn in school can really make a difference in the world.

I've also noticed a change in myself. I am going to school each day with a much more positive attitude than I had before I started the badge system, and I simply feel better about the work I am doing in my students' lives. I don't feel as if I'm dragging students through a series of obstacles to get them through the school year—instead, I feel like I'm opening doors for them and watching them run through on their own.

I'm not the only one who has found success with the system, either. I have shared my ideas at various conferences and through conversation, and I know of many teachers throughout the United States, Canada, and Latin America who are trying the system.

One school in Peru has been so pleased with the results that they are considering a schoolwide transition to the badge system. In addition to the overall success I've had with the program, there have also been a few individual students whose stories stick with me. These stories confirmed that the system was accomplishing exactly what it had been designed to do.

The first student to come to mind was Austin. After I'd been running my new and challenging tech curriculum and tech clubs for a few years, Austin signed up to be in my newly formed morning news podcasting club. As standard procedure, I asked why he wanted to be part of the morning news team on the application. His answer was that he wanted to get over his "shyness problem."

As things developed with the morning news podcast, this shy fifth grade student ended up expanding my mind as to what I thought young students were capable of—just as Dr. Tyson promised me they would. In fact, he inspired me to write this book.

Austin had been trained in how to use our little elementary school's news podcasting studio and was really getting the hang of being a newscaster. His shyness seemed to be disappearing with every chance he got to be behind the mic.

Then one Wednesday it happened. It was a cold December morning in 2009, and Austin had turned up at his usual time to do the morning news. His fourth grade sound tech had cued up all the sound effects, checked the mics, and was now ready for the show to start at precisely 8:05 a.m. Meanwhile, Austin had prepared the normal script, complete with the lunch recess weather forecast, the hot lunch menu, birthdays, and so on.

At 8:05 a.m., the sound tech counted down, 5 … 4 … and then silently turned up the mics as her finger signaled for him to start.

What came out of this fifth grader's mouth was amazing. He was off script and totally ad-libbing his show. Sure, he was still covering the news, birthdays, and so on., but he was doing it *his* way. As I watched his sound tech scramble to keep up, a smile grew across my face as I realized he got it; he had found something that he was really good at, and he knew it.

The show ended, he hung up his headphones and walked out of the studio to be the new shining star of our elementary school. All I could do was smile as he walked off to his first-period class.

It was then when I found out that the most rewarding part of teaching is when you see a child find a passion for something that they never knew they had. This is what great skill-based projects can do for our students.

I must admit that I was worried at the beginning of my new badge program about using extrinsic motivation to motivate the students to learn. Would the students just do the program to get the badge and in the end not really care about anything more? Also, what about the student who likes to take things slowly—would he be teased because he only has two badges while his classmates have eight?

It turns out that my fears were unfounded. The truth was that my students soon forgot about the actual badge and instead focused on the cool things that they were learning to do on their iPads. Sure, they loved getting the badges, but more importantly, they connected to the cause and charity that my badge program supported. The badge primes the pump and gives them the energy to try something new and perhaps difficult.

I remember one of the lead singers from the first iPad band talking to me about how happy she was that her voice was going to help get books for students that didn't have any. She felt like she could do her part to make her world a better place. I know it sounds corny, but she had done so much research on the problem of illiteracy in the world that she told everyone one she could talk to that they should buy a ticket to see her perform and help buy some books for kids in Nicaragua to learn to read. Just before her mom fixed her hair and put on a little makeup, she said to me, "Mr. Flick, I never thought I would ever be able to sing in front of people and I never thought that I could make a difference, but tonight, both things are going to happen." After her song, when the crowd was in disbelief of her amazing performance, and she still had the mic in her hand, she told them to go over and fill the donation jar.

The motivation of getting a badge got her to try the digital music badge, but soon she was doing it for so much more.

CHAPTER NINE

Frequently Asked Questions

YOU HAVE JUST BEEN through a crash course on badging and you may be feeling a mixture of things: excitement, trepidation, information overload … And naturally you may have questions. Questions are an important part of the learning process. In my presentations and conversations about badging I have been asked a wide array of questions. I share some of them below so you can learn from what others have asked with regard to badging.

Q. How can I determine whether a student passes my class?

A. A badge program should not enable students to progress academically without gaining skills. In fact, the badge program should stop this from happening by making it impossible for students to squeak by with low grades and only partial mastery of the skills they need. However, the badge program is also designed to allow students to work at their own pace. To determine if a student has passed your class, you need to set the number of badges needed to pass the class. I only require my students to pass all the level 1 badges and then one required badge from levels 2 and 3. All the other badges are optional. I have noticed that I get the best work when students are not forced to do a badge.

Q. How can I use this system if my school insists on grades?

A. Building on the previous question, many of us not only need to determine if students are passing our class or our grade level, but also need to designate a letter grade to symbolize their achievement. When I transitioned from badges to traditional grades, I just made a scale. For example, to get an A in my class, the student would have to complete at least one level 4 badge.

Q. How can we motivate students to continue pursuing badges once they have reached the passing level?

A. As I wrote earlier in this book, the badges are only a way to reward and keep score—the student should really want to continue because they enjoy the challenges. If students are reluctant to voluntarily try other badge, then you need to rethink your challenges. My iBand badge is not required, but I have students lined up to try and earn it.

Q. I like the idea of badges, but I'm not ready to take the plunge. How can I begin to incorporate badging in my current teaching?

A. Start by adding a few option challenges. Use them as an extension to your regular lesson. "Here is what you will need to get a good grade for this unit—but if you're interested in more, then I have a challenge for you." Limit it to the first four or five students to add a sense of urgency.

Q. I can see my students becoming so excited about working on the badge artifacts that they might take time way from other classes and test preparation. What advice do you have?

A. This one is easy—only allow them to work on their badges at home. You can also use it as a reward: "Get your work done and I'll let you work on your badges for the remainder of the period."

Q. What if a student isn't motivated to pursue badges? What are the consequences if there are no grades?

A. Although the badge program inspires intrinsic motivation in many students, many teachers can picture a certain student or two taking advantage of the system's freedom and choice. "I don't feel like starting another badge today," you might imagine them saying, or "I am satisfied by getting to level 2. I don't think I'm going to go any higher." Depending on how you are correlating grades to the badge system, the threat of a low or failing grade may not be at your disposal.

Q. You mentioned earlier in the book that your system could be adapted and used in an entire department or by the entire school. Could you explain how that could be done?

A. It really comes down to scalability. A grade level or department could follow the same process and come up with the list of skills that every student should have for the best chance of success. Then those skills could be divided into levels and badges made. Most schools already have a system for rewarding those students who demonstrate good qualities like attendance, kindness, and leadership. But now, instead of a certificate, they earn a badge from their principal.

Q. Tell me more about your role in your school.

A. I was in charge of the media center and technology for my elementary school, so I would see each K–5 class for one hour a week. During their hour in my class, they might work on an assignment from their teacher. For example, their teacher might send her students to my media center to work on a project about the human body. But most times they would work on badges during their time in the media center. Badges were always the "Plan B" if their time in my media center was not needed for a classroom project.

Q. How much technology do you have at your school?

A. For most of the examples you see in this book, the students each had a netbook (1:1), and I had eight iPads for the students to check out.

References

Apple, Inc. (2010). Challenge based learning: A classroom guide. Retrieved from: http://www.apple.com/br/education/docs/CBL_Classroom_Guide_Jan_2011.pdf

Bhoje, G. (2015). *The Importance of Motivation in an Educational Environment*. New Delhi: Laxmi Publications

Crockett, L., Jukes, I., & Churches, A. (2011). *Literacy is not enough: 21st-century fluencies for the digital age*. Kelowna, B.C.: 21st Century Fluency Project.

Digital Promise. (2014). Developing rigorous, reputable micro-credentials. Retrieved from: http://digitalpromise.org/2014/04/04/

Klopfer, Osterweil, & Salen. (2009). Moving learning games forward. Retrieved from: http://education.mit.edu/wp-content/uploads/2015/01/MovingLearningGamesForward_EdArcade.pdf

LaPlante, L. 2013. Hackschooling makes me happy. TedX University of Nevada